GETTING ON THE Road To Recovery:

Your Step-By-Step Guide To Auto Accident Claims

Joshua Moody, Esq.

Jacobs & Whitehall
9600 Escarpment Blvd
Suite 745-282
Austin, TX 78749
www.jacobsandwhitehall.com

Ordering Information:

Quantity sales. Special discounts are available on quantity purchases by corporations, associations, and others. For details, contact the publisher at the address above.

Orders by U.S. trade bookstores and wholesalers. Please contact Jacobs & Whitehall: Tel: (888) 570-7338 or visit www.jacobsandwhitehall.com.

Printed in the United States of America

Published in 2024

ISBN: 978-1-963063-15-8

PREFACE

This book aims to demystify the legal system, particularly focusing on personal injury law. It is important to note that this text does not provide legal advice or serve as a step-by-step guide for handling cases. Instead, it seeks to lay the foundational concepts of personal injury law, highlighting that every case is unique and influenced by a multitude of factors, both large and small.

Confidentiality is crucial in the attorney-client relationship, and the information shared in confidence can significantly impact how a case is approached. In a time when many believe they can simply "Google" legal information, this book serves as an accessible introduction. My hope is that, should you ever find yourself in need of legal counsel, you will be better informed for your first meeting with an attorney.

Dedication

To Mari.

Disclaimer

This publication is intended to be used for educational purposes only. No legal advice is being given, and no attorney-client relationship is intended to be created by reading this material. The author assumes no liability for any errors or omissions or for how this book or its contents are used or interpreted, or for any consequences resulting directly or indirectly from the use of this book. For legal or any other advice, please consult an experienced attorney or the appropriate expert, who is aware of the specific facts of your case and is knowledgeable in the law in your jurisdiction.

Moody Law

17768 Wika Rd #201,
Apple Valley, CA 92307
(760) 867-3300
www.moodylawyer.com

TESTIMONIALS

"The office provides the best litigation and representation in the Inland Empire. Attorney Moody is a great communicator, he is organized and an outstanding litigator. He truly prepares himself before court hearings and keeps his clients informed. He is outstanding in court and a great litigator. He cares about his clients' cases and the client truly feels important since Moody takes great care of his clients. I wouldn't recommend anyone else or any other law firm to manage my case. Great job Mr. Moody!!!"

— Armando Castillo

****

"My experience with Moody and Associates was exceptional. He was very informative and kept in close contact. At no point was I out of the loop as to the status of my case. I have referred several friends and family who also had nothing but great things to say about Moody and Associates. I would definitely recommend them to anyone needing assistance in difficult times."

— Timothy Visosky

****

"After my mom had an incident I called Mr. Moody and set an appointment up for her. He was very attentive and helpful with her case! We are extremely thankful we found this attorney. Mr. Moody and his secretary were on top of it and always so nice. I highly recommend this attorney to anyone looking for one.

They listen and communicate with you throughout the whole process keeping you in the loop. They went above and beyond for my mom. We are extremely happy with the outcome of her case!"

– Selina Clark

****

"If you require quality legal representation, I highly recommend Attorney Joshua Moody. He is responsive, and professional, and brings a wealth of knowledge and experience to his cases; he truly cares about his clients. I've referred several of my friends and colleagues to his office and will continue to do so."

– Dayna LaFond

****

"I came to Joshua Moody for help and he did just that, he helped me. He gave me a piece of mind knowing my case was in the right hands. I am so grateful for my outcome in court and I owe it all to Josh for representing me and really caring about my needs and worries. I highly recommend Joshua Moody."

– Rebecca Mendoza

****

Table of Contents

i.	Preface	3
ii.	Dedication	4
iii.	Disclaimer	5
iv.	Testimonials	6
v.	Table of Contents	8
vi.	About The Author	10
1.	What To Do At The Scene Of An Accident	15
2.	Common Misconceptions & Mistakes	21
3.	In The Aftermath: When To Contact An Attorney & How To Handle Claims Adjusters	27
4.	Filing A Claim Vs. Filing A Lawsuit	32

5. **Understanding Settlements & Claim Value** 38

6. **The Trial Process** 45

7. **Uninsured Motorist Claims** 52

8. **Wrongful Death Claims** 58

9. **Practical Tips & Closing Remarks** 65

vii. **Index** 72

viii. **Notes** 75

About The Author

My journey into personal injury law began with nearly two decades of service as a deputy sheriff in Apple Valley, California, where I currently practice law. During my time as a deputy, I investigated countless car accidents, gaining a deep and practical understanding of the California Vehicle Code. This experience provided me with unique insights into fault, liability, and how the vehicle code is constructed and applied in real-world situations.

Many people, including some attorneys, often overlook critical details in the vehicle code that can be pivotal in proving negligence per se—a legal doctrine in California where a violation of the vehicle code can establish fault. I've seen firsthand how a simple, often-forgotten section of the code can make a significant difference in proving liability in a personal injury case. This has reinforced a core belief of mine: working with an attorney who can fully leverage the vehicle code is crucial, regardless of any upfront savings you might consider.

My background gives me a unique perspective that extends far beyond relying solely on police reports. While these reports can be useful tools, they are by no means the final word on fault in an accident. Having reviewed countless cases, I've seen numerous instances where the conclusions in reports were incorrect—sometimes in ways that actually benefit my clients.

My understanding of statutory construction and the application of traffic laws allows me to critically assess cases, often uncovering key details that others miss. This ability has enabled me to take on cases that other attorneys may have dropped due to an unfavorable police report, only to discover that the officer, and consequently the insurance company, may have been mistaken in their assessment.

After my career in law enforcement, I transitioned to law and worked for a personal injury firm before opening my own practice. This shift in focus—from determining fault in an accident to addressing the resulting injuries and ensuring fair compensation for my clients—has allowed me to effectively advocate for those I represent, drawing on my deep understanding of both the investigative and legal aspects of car accidents.

Interestingly, personal injury law was not initially the area I envisioned myself pursuing. It wasn't until I started working at another law firm that my perspective began to change. Handling compelling cases and participating in meaningful trials showed me the profound impact injuries can have on a person's life. These injuries, even those that may seem minor to an outsider, are often deeply significant to those who are suffering. Helping clients navigate their recovery became immensely fulfilling for me.

There's a common misconception that if you are injured in an accident, compensation is automatic, and everything will be set right. However, the reality is far more complex. Severe injuries, such as the loss of a limb or a loved one, present immense challenges—perhaps the hardest experiences one can go through. Being able to assist people during such difficult times, and helping them find some semblance of justice or relief, is what ultimately drew me to personal injury law and continues to fuel my passion for this work.

My time is often limited, making it challenging to delve deeply into all the intricacies of personal injury law, especially when trying to reach those who aren't already familiar with this area. I wrote this book for anyone who might be considering hiring an attorney, knows someone going through a similar situation, or is already in the midst of it and could benefit from a more thorough understanding of the process and their case.

People absorb information in different ways—some by listening, others by reading, or even by doing.

This book allows readers to grasp the details at their own pace. For those who find reading helps them better understand concepts, I hope this book will be particularly useful.

My aim is for readers to come away with a better understanding of how the legal system works and how cases progress through it. If you gain even a little more insight into what we do and why we do it, then this book will have served its purpose. My goal is to make the process more transparent, helping you feel more informed and empowered as you navigate these challenges.

CHAPTER 1

WHAT TO DO AT THE SCENE OF AN ACCIDENT

Immediately After An Accident

The most important thing to do immediately after an accident is to ensure that everyone involved is safe. Your priority should always be to check for injuries and, if needed, call emergency services as quickly as possible. This could make all the difference in preventing further harm and saving lives. Once you are certain that everyone is safe, shift your focus to preserving the accident scene.

Since you likely carry a smartphone with you, take as many pictures as possible to document the scene. Do not limit your photos to just your own vehicle. Be sure to capture images of the other vehicles involved as well. This is crucial for proving the facts of the accident, especially by clearly showing all the damage incurred to the other vehicle. These photos can help reconstruct the accident and may reveal discrepancies if the other party is not entirely truthful about what happened.

Do not stop here, though. Take pictures of the surrounding area, including the intersection, street, or any skid marks or debris on the road. These details can be equally important. If you've never been involved in an accident, there is a good chance you won't realize that emergency responders unintentionally alter the scene upon arriving at it. Their job is to preserve life, and so they are understandably focused on doing that. This oftentimes entails moving vehicles and disturbing evidence as they work. When I was a deputy, we would often call the fire department the Evidence Eradication Team because of their tendency to inadvertently erase evidence simply by doing their job.

Remember, even though it is natural to be concerned about the damage to your own car, capturing the full context of the scene can significantly impact the outcome of your case. Following these steps, even in a stressful situation, can make all the difference later should your claim become a lawsuit and go to court.

Key Insights At A Car Crash Scene From A Traffic Investigator's Perspective

Your health and well-being, as well as that of others involved, should be your top priority immediately after you've been involved in an accident. No amount of compensation can truly make up for the pain, suffering, or loss that you may endure. If you could go back and prevent the accident, you undoubtedly would because, chances are, whatever you may win in compensation simply isn't worth the ordeal. This is why seeking medical attention immediately after an accident is so critical—it ensures that your health is prioritized and that any injuries are properly documented.

Preserving evidence at the scene is also essential for building a strong case. This is not just about establishing fault or liability, although that is a significant part of it. It is especially important if your injuries are serious, and your case eventually goes to trial, mediation, or arbitration.

During the legal process, particularly in the discovery phase, both sides will exchange evidence, including photographs and other documentation from the scene. The evidence you preserve now can make a significant difference in the outcome of your case, helping to support your claims and counter any arguments the opposing side makes.

One of the most important things to remember is not to admit liability at the scene. Beyond that, avoid discussing who might be at fault. When the police arrive, simply provide them with a clear account of what happened—what you saw and experienced—without trying to fill in any gaps or making assumptions. Let the professionals determine liability because anything you say, even an innocent apology like, "I didn't see you," could be interpreted as an admission of fault, which might not even be accurate.

Beyond this, make sure to document who was driving. This can be crucial, especially in cases where there are multiple passengers and questions about who was driving the other vehicle. It is not uncommon for someone with a suspended license, for instance, to claim they were not driving when they were. Documenting these details early on will help you avoid tricky issues later.

Writing down the sequence of events as soon as possible after an accident can be incredibly valuable. I usually advise clients to do this when they come into the office, but if you can jot down details at the scene or shortly thereafter, it is even better. Recording things like the other driver's license plate, the name they provided, and your own recollection of events can help ensure you do not forget critical details. You might think you will remember everything. However, as time goes on, minor details will be forgotten months, or even years later.

However, keep in mind that anything you write down could potentially be used as evidence in your case. If you make notes at the scene, those notes might be accessed during legal proceedings. On the other hand, if you take notes for your attorney once you are in my office, those are generally protected under attorney-client privilege, meaning they can't be used against you. So, while it is a good idea to document everything, be mindful of how and when you do it.

CHAPTER 2

COMMON MISCONCEPTIONS & MISTAKES

Common Misconceptions Surrounding Personal Injury

One of the most common misconceptions people have when they come to us is believing that because they were innocently minding their own business when they got injured, the responsible party will automatically cover everything and make things right. Unfortunately, that is not usually how it works. Even if the other party admits liability, it does not mean they will pay the full amount you may deserve. Insurance companies often try to minimize the payout. Remember, they are a business first. Also, if everyone was fully compensated after an accident, there would be no personal injury attorneys, and I would be out of business! Think about how many personal injury attorney ads you see on television and billboards. This business exists *because* insurance companies do not initially fully pay out injured parties.

Another common misconception is about medical treatment. People often come in weeks or months after the incident, saying they need medical treatment, expecting the other party to cover those expenses. The reality is that the responsible party's insurance isn't obligated to help you with medical treatment upfront. You will need to find and pay for your own treatment initially, which can be financially difficult for many people.

Finally, another significant misconception people have is the idea that you won't have to pay anyone else out of your settlement. The truth is that various parties, including your health insurance company, might try to claim a portion of your settlement. These are called subrogation claims, and part of our job as your attorney is to handle these claims and minimize the amount that goes out from your settlement to these other parties.

Understanding these misconceptions will help you set realistic expectations as you navigate the complexities of your personal injury law case.

Common Mistakes People Make After An Accident

Perhaps the most common mistake people make after an accident is not properly documenting the scene. They might spend a lot of time focusing on the damage to their own car but neglect to gather vital information about the other vehicle involved. Proper documentation includes taking photos, getting witness statements, and noting important details about the accident's circumstances.

Another significant mistake is putting off contacting an attorney. Many people wait too long, assuming the insurance company will handle everything fairly. This misconception can lead to missed opportunities for proper legal guidance and support. Promptly contacting an attorney ensures you have someone looking out for your best interests from the start.

A third common mistake is not documenting your injuries in a timely manner. People often wait for the insurance company to take action, expecting them to arrange medical treatment. This rarely happens, if at all. It is critical to seek medical attention immediately after your accident and keep thorough records of all treatments and diagnoses.

Some people also make the mistake of trying to handle the case themselves, thinking they can find a higher payout by avoiding legal fees. While some might manage this successfully, it often leads to a lower settlement. If maximizing your settlement is important, having an attorney on your side will make a significant difference. Attorneys are experienced in negotiating with insurance companies and ensuring that all aspects of your case are thoroughly addressed.

The takeaway? Act quickly and seek professional advice to protect your interests and secure the best possible outcome you can. My philosophy is very simple. I want all my clients to get more money in their pocket than if they handled the case themselves or went with a different attorney.

Avoiding Pitfalls

If you want to avoid the most common pitfalls of the personal injury claims process, reach into your pocket! Your phone's camera is arguably the best tool you have after an accident. It is an all-in-one device for documenting the accident scene. Take photos of both vehicles, the surrounding area, any visible injuries, and anything else that might be relevant. This visual evidence will be a big help in your case later on.

Second, contact an attorney as soon as possible. Even if you are at the hospital, do not hesitate to reach out. Many people with serious injuries do this, but it is just as important if you have less severe injuries like back or neck pain. Once you are able to leave the hospital, give our firm a call immediately. Our phones are on 24/7, 365 days a year, and we can start helping you right away[1]. By signing up with us, you'll receive our literature, guidelines, and advice promptly, which can help you navigate the next steps.

Also, if you are at the hospital or are unable to come to our office, we can come to you or we can send you all the documents to your phone. It is that simple.

So, remember, the two biggest things you can do to avoid common pitfalls are to use your camera and contact an attorney as soon as possible. Do not forget them!

---

[1] You can reach Moody Law, located in Apple Valley, California at any time for a free consultation by calling (760) 867-3300 or visiting www.moodylawyer.com. We would be happy to speak with you about your case.

CHAPTER 3

IN THE AFTERMATH: WHEN TO CONTACT AN ATTORNEY & HOW TO HANDLE CLAIMS ADJUSTERS

Contacting A Personal Injury Attorney After An Accident

You should contact a personal injury attorney immediately after your accident. There is really no such thing as contacting an attorney "too soon"—I've had clients reach out from the hospital or call on the same day as the accident. The sooner you involve an attorney, the better it is for preserving evidence.

Whether it is securing a police report, identifying witnesses, or obtaining red-light camera footage, early action can make a significant difference in your case.

While it is possible to contact an attorney later—sometimes even up to two years after the accident—the risks increase dramatically the longer you wait. Important evidence might be lost, or witnesses might become harder to locate. Although cases involving significant injuries with substantial documentation might still be viable for a claim later, it is always best to act quickly. This is why our phones are open 24/7, so we can assist you immediately[2], even if you are still in the hospital.

Why Partner With An Attorney

My job as your attorney is to get you as much money as possible. Most importantly, it is to ensure you have the most money in your pocket at the end of the

---

[2] You can call Moody Law for a free consultation at any time by dialing (760) 867-3300 or visiting www.moodylawyer.com. We're here to help.

case. On the other hand, the claims adjuster's job is to protect *their* client—the person who caused your injuries—and to settle the case as cheaply as possible. That is what you need to understand about a claims adjuster: their job is to represent their client, just as my job is to represent you.

There is a common misconception that the claims adjuster will hand over the maximum amount of money simply because their client is at fault. That is simply not reality. The adjuster does not owe you any loyalty or duty to be fair. While they must be truthful and cannot lie to you, they are not obligated to offer you the maximum compensation available.

Adjusters have a duty to act in good faith, but what does that mean? It means that if they value a case in a certain range, they will make you an offer based on that "good faith" valuation? But what if they did not consider all the facts? What if they did not get all the evidence? What if they put a higher value on a different injury and a lower value on another?

It is important to realize this about claims adjusters. This is why you need someone on your side who has quality experience. In my line of work, I often encounter the same adjusters, so I have a good sense of who is straightforward and who might try to settle for less than they should. Understanding the role of the claims adjuster is crucial.

An attorney's strong suit is finding liability—identifying where the other party may be at fault. The adjuster is not going to volunteer information that might indicate their client has some liability that has not been noticed. Adjusters do not owe you a duty to point out potential weaknesses in their client's case. That is why it is so important to remember that the claims adjuster represents the person who hit you; they are not looking out for you. If they must pay you, they will, but their goal is to do so at the lowest cost possible, which is why my job is to get you the most money possible. It is two competing interests going head-to-head in an adversarial relationship.

Many people assume that if they were hit and injured, the insurance company will just pay them what is fair. While they might pay you, they are also trying to do so as cheaply as possible. This is why having an attorney is so important. People often get frustrated, but it is important not to get angry at the adjuster for doing their job, just as you would not get angry at me for trying to get you the most compensation.

This system is set up in such a way that personal injury law is not an exact science. The liability aspect might have some scientific elements, but determining the value of a case is more of an art. Both sides operate within a range: the adjuster is aiming for the low end, and we are aiming for the high end. Our job is to push for the highest possible settlement within *our* range, while the adjuster tries to keep it at the low end. Understanding this dynamic is key to navigating the process effectively.

CHAPTER 4

FILING A CLAIM VS. FILING A LAWSUIT

The Key Differences Between Filing A Claim And A Lawsuit

Filing a claim typically precedes a lawsuit, though it is not mandatory. In about 90% of cases, a claim is filed first. A claim is essentially a written notice to the insurance company, stating that my client has been injured, their vehicle has been damaged, and some other harm has occurred. This is a more informal process, aimed at resolving the issue before escalating to a lawsuit. Settling the matter at this stage is often preferable because it saves both time and money. Lawsuits, on the other hand, can be expensive, so it is best to attempt to resolve your case at the lowest level possible.

In California, there is a two-year statute of limitation, which gives you time to settle the issue before needing to file a lawsuit. This period also allows for medical treatment and recovery, so you can fully assess the extent of your injuries before deciding to take legal action.

A lawsuit becomes necessary when common ground cannot be found, and neither party is satisfied with the outcome of the claim process. As the plaintiff, we initiate the lawsuit by filing a complaint and summons, which effectively orders the defendant to court. This is done through the local court—in our county, typically in San Bernardino. Once the lawsuit is filed, the defendant is served, and in personal injury cases, they usually pass the lawsuit to their insurance company, which then handles the case.

Filing a lawsuit involves various costs, including locating the defendant, serving them with the lawsuit, and processing the case. Unlike a claim, a lawsuit grants you specific entitlements and rights. Once the necessary paperwork is completed, you can summon the defendant for a deposition and call their experts into depositions. Similarly, the defendant has rights—they can subpoena you for a deposition, request your medical records, and obtain your medical history.

In short, the difference between a claim and a lawsuit lies not only in the financial cost but also in the rights and responsibilities involved. Filing a lawsuit brings certain entitlements, but it also means giving up some control and taking on additional responsibilities.

Filing A Personal Injury Claim

When you have decided you want to move forward with filing a claim, the first thing we do is notify everyone involved that we represent you. This includes informing the other party's insurance company, any other relevant insurance companies, your health insurance provider, and any doctors you might be seeing. By putting everyone on notice that you are represented, we prevent them from contacting you directly. This also allows us to handle your bills and gather all necessary evidence on your behalf.

Next, the defense adjuster will acknowledge our representation and begin communicating with us directly. During this time, your case will proceed with the necessary medical treatments, which could take anywhere from a few weeks to several months or even longer, depending on the extent of your injuries.

Once your treatment is complete, we gather all your medical records, bills, and related documents. We then review everything and contact you to discuss the case's value. At this point, we prepare what we call a "demand package," which we send to the insurance adjuster. This package outlines how much we believe your case is worth and what we are seeking to avoid litigation.

From there, the defense adjuster typically responds with a counteroffer, and the process becomes a negotiation. Our goal during this stage is to reach a settlement that reflects the true value of your case without needing to escalate to a lawsuit.

The Importance Of Ongoing Medical Care

Ongoing medical care is important for your recovery – and because it documents and demonstrates the injuries you have sustained. As you receive treatment, your doctors make detailed notes and entries in your medical records that will later be subpoenaed or turned over as evidence to support your claim.

The unfortunate reality is that anyone who is injured in an accident can say, "My back hurts," or "My neck hurts," but verbal descriptions alone often do not resonate with jurors or others involved in the case. Even more severe injuries like lost limbs or broken bones often sound the same when merely spoken about before a jury. This is because jurors and others often do not fully grasp the severity just from words. Pain descriptions blur together when people hear the same thing many times. However, seeing your injuries documented in medical charts or on X-rays generally carries much more weight with a jury.

This tangible evidence is why ongoing medical treatment is truly essential. The reason is simple: without knowing the full extent of your injuries and the associated medical costs, we cannot accurately determine the value of your case. In fact, filing a claim too early can work against you. If we do not have all the necessary information, the defense might offer a settlement based on incomplete data, which could be far less than what you are entitled to. If you settle early on in your case and later discover you need additional treatment, such as surgery, you may have already limited your ability to receive adequate compensation.

While many people assume that we will file a lawsuit immediately after they come in, that is often times not the case. We wait until you have completed your treatment and have all your medical records and bills in hand. This approach ensures that we have a complete understanding of your injuries and can advocate for the total amount of compensation you deserve.

CHAPTER 5

UNDERSTANDING SETTLEMENTS & CLAIM VALUE

Calculating The Value Of A Personal Injury Claim

The value of a personal injury claim is primarily based on two factors: the amount of your medical bills and the extent of your injuries. These are the key elements that determine the worth of your case. While the reason for the accident, such as the defendant being distracted by a cell phone, might influence perceptions, it generally does not directly affect the value of the case. For instance, whether the defendant was fiddling with the radio or simply did not see you, the value is mostly driven by the injuries and costs involved. These factors can help influence a jury and make the defendant less sympathetic, but there are specific jury instructions the jury must follow to reach a verdict for compensation.

To that end, medical documentation, such as MRI or X-ray results, stands out as being especially significant. For example, in cases involving concussions or traumatic brain injuries (TBI), seeing the actual MRI images and their details is incredibly powerful. This tangible evidence can greatly impact the value of your case, driving home the severity and reality of the injuries you've suffered.

Damages

The most common types of recovery in personal injury cases are *economic* and *noneconomic damages. Economic damages* include medical expenses and *lost wages*. Medical expenses can be broken down into past medical expenses—expenses you've already incurred—and future medical expenses—anticipated costs for ongoing treatment. Lost wages is yet another form of compensation that covers income lost due to the injury, which can also be divided into past lost wages and future lost earnings.

Furthermore, *noneconomic damages,* often referred to as *pain and suffering,* cover compensation for the physical pain and emotional distress caused by the injury. These, too, can be categorized into past noneconomic damages—pain and suffering experienced up to the present—and future noneconomic damages—anticipated ongoing pain and suffering.

My Approach To The Settlement Negotiation Process

When it comes to settlement negotiations, I believe that the key to success lies in keeping an open mind. Approaching the process without a preconceived notion or rigid belief about the case's value is crucial. More important, *listening* is essential because it allows you to hear the other side's arguments, strengths, and weaknesses. Just because the other side presents something does not mean it is true or accurate. True skill in negotiation lies in discerning between valid points and weaker arguments while staying firmly grounded in the strengths of your case.

My strategy is to start negotiations in an open-ended manner. Doing so means I increase the likelihood of keeping the conversation fluid and allowing for the discovery of new information that might be important to the case. I do my best not to get stuck in a single way of thinking, as cases can often take unexpected turns during negotiations. Being too focused on a particular outcome or approach can lead to missed opportunities or even significantly undervaluing the case.

A significant part of my preparation involves staying up to date on recent jury verdicts and settlements. I use specialized software and databases to understand how cases like yours have been valued in the past. This information is vital when determining whether to settle or proceed to trial. Additionally, these tools help me create a clear picture of what you could expect to receive today versus the potential outcomes if we go to court.

Ultimately, *the decision on whether to settle or go to court rests with you, the client*. My role is to provide you with all the information you need to make an informed decision. This includes running the numbers, considering the costs, and analyzing the risks. Settlement negotiations are a complex and dynamic process, but by staying flexible, informed, and client focused, I aim to achieve the best possible outcome for each case.

Insurance Subrogation

When you are involved in an accident and your health insurance covers your medical bills, it is important to be aware that your insurance company may be entitled to a portion of any settlement or award you receive. This process is known as subrogation.

In California, if you have health insurance—whether it is through a private provider, Medicare, or

Medi-Cal—your insurer has the right to be reimbursed from your settlement for the expenses they covered on your behalf. This means that a portion of the money you receive may go back to your insurance company to cover the costs of your medical treatment.

For example, if you are in a car accident and require emergency services, such as an ambulance ride to the hospital and overnight medical care, your health insurance will likely cover those costs initially. However, once you receive a settlement or judgment for your injuries, your insurance provider will seek reimbursement.

California law requires that the state gets paid first in subrogation claims. This can come as a surprise to many people who receive a large settlement, only to find the state is claiming a portion of it.

My role as your attorney is to minimize the amount that your insurance provider or the state takes from your settlement, ensuring that more of this money stays in your pocket. To do this, we negotiate with the insurance companies to reduce the amount they seek in subrogation, which can significantly impact the final amount you receive.

Our work is not just about securing the highest possible settlement from the insurance company—it also involves considering the doctors and medical providers who treated you after the accident. You did not choose to be taken by ambulance or admitted to the ER, but those expenses are still subject to subrogation. Understanding this is key when deciding whether to accept a settlement or to file a lawsuit.

CHAPTER 6

THE TRIAL PROCESS

Escalating Your Claim To A Lawsuit

Typically, a lawsuit is filed close to the statute of limitation to preserve your case. If you let the statute of limitations expire, you lose your right to pursue the case, and the other party is no longer obligated to pay anything. Filing a lawsuit closer to the deadline is common, especially if a settlement has not been reached.

Another reason lawsuits are often filed closer to the statute of limitations is due to the time needed for medical treatment and the collection of billing records and other necessary documentation. This can take time—sometimes 30 to 45 days or longer—so it is often best to wait until all the information is gathered.

In some cases, we file lawsuits earlier, particularly in cases with disputed liability. If the defense denies fault and refuses to negotiate, we might file sooner to push the case forward. This also happens in larger cases involving serious injuries or death, where the defense wants to delve deeper into the personal lives and medical histories of those involved.

Considering filing a lawsuit usually occurs a few months before the statute of limitations expire, and it becomes clear that the case cannot be resolved through settlement. At that point, we evaluate the case, discuss the settlement offer with our client, and decide whether to accept the offer or move forward with a lawsuit. The decision to proceed to trial is typically made after thorough analysis, considering the potential costs and benefits.

The Trial Process

The trial process for a personal injury case is long and demanding. More than this, legal fees typically explode once a lawsuit is initiated, making it quite expensive. This is not unique to our firm—it is true for all attorneys because the work involved becomes significantly more involved and intense.

Before going to trial, California law requires that you attempt to resolve your case through mediation or a settlement conference, even if you would prefer not to. A judge will typically order this as a part of the process. Preparing for this is essential, and sometimes it is beneficial.

Once you file a lawsuit, the process begins with serving the defendant. In most personal injury cases, the defendant will turn the lawsuit over to their insurance company, which will then assign it to a law firm, either in-house or external.

From there, the discovery phase starts, where both sides gather and share evidence. This includes depositions, where the involved parties are questioned under oath. You have the right to depose the defendant, any other occupants of the vehicle, and witnesses. The defense will likely depose you, any witnesses on your side, and possibly the police officer who responded to the accident.

Medical experts also play a key role at this point in the process. Your doctors may be deposed, and the defense will often bring in their own medical experts to challenge the extent of your injuries. Both sides may also employ an accident reconstructionist to present different interpretations of how the accident occurred.

Once all evidence has been gathered, exchanged, and reviewed, and all attempts at settlement have been exhausted, the case will proceed to trial. That is when the jury trial officially begins, where both sides present their arguments, and a verdict is eventually reached.

Pros And Cons Of Going To Trial

When considering whether to go to trial, it is essential to weigh the potential benefits and drawbacks. This list is not exhaustive, but will nevertheless give you a solid foundation to make an informed decision when you are confronted with the need to do so.

Pros

- **Potential For Higher Compensation**

One of the most significant advantages of going to trial is the possibility of securing a larger financial award. Trials can result in higher payouts than settlements because a jury might award more in damages than what was offered during negotiations.

- **Confronting The Responsible Party**

Going to trial allows you to directly face the person or entity that caused your injuries. For some, this is an important part of the healing process and can provide a deeper, more subjective sense of justice.

- **Enforcing Legal Rights**

In a trial, both sides are required to adhere strictly to legal procedures, which means the opposing party must provide all necessary evidence and make their client available for questioning. This can be beneficial if you feel the other side has been withholding information.

Cons

- **Financial Costs**

Trial is expensive. The legal fees increase significantly out of the gate, and this only continues the longer the case drags on. Even if you win a larger award, the expenses associated with going to trial can dramatically eat into that amount, sometimes leaving you with less money than you would have received in a settlement.

- **Risk Of A Lower Award**

There is also the risk that the jury may award less than what was offered during settlement negotiations. If this happens, you could end up with a smaller amount than if you had settled.

- **Time And Emotional Toll**

Trial prep can take a long time, sometimes stretching over several years. This process can be emotionally draining and stressful, especially if the outcome is uncertain.

Ultimately, the decision to go to trial depends on what is most important to *you*. If you prioritize a higher potential payout or the chance to confront the responsible party, going to trial might be the right choice. However, if your goal is to maximize the amount of money in your pocket as quickly as possible, a settlement may be more prudent. There is no one-size-fits-all answer. Your case is unique, and your decision should be based on your specific circumstances and priorities.

CHAPTER 7

UNINSURED MOTORIST CLAIMS

Navigating Accidents With Uninsured Or Underinsured Motorists

Living in California, it is crucial to understand the importance of protecting yourself against uninsured and underinsured motorists. Unfortunately, there are a significant number of drivers on the road who either do not have insurance, do not hold a valid license, or are driving vehicles that are barely roadworthy. If you do not take proactive steps to protect yourself, you could be left without compensation for injuries or damages if you are involved in an accident with one of these drivers.

One of the best ways to protect yourself is by purchasing Uninsured Motorist (UM) Coverage through your insurance company. This coverage steps in if you are hit by someone who does not have insurance, and you suffer injuries as a result. This ensures you have a safety net in place should you find yourself in an accident with one of these types of drivers.

How Does UM/UIM Coverage Work?

Underinsured Motorist (UIM) Coverage comes into play when the at-fault driver has insurance, but it is not enough to cover the damages you have sustained. In a struggling economy, one of the first bills people stop paying or reduce is their insurance premiums. Unfortunately, there are countless cases where the at-fault driver simply does not have insurance, leaving you to rely on your own coverage.

In California, the current minimum liability coverage is $15,000 per person and $30,000 per accident. This amount may be insufficient in cases of severe injury or significant damage. Purchasing UIM coverage is a way to ensure that you have additional resources available if the at-fault driver's policy does not cover your losses.

One of the biggest challenges in uninsured motorist cases is the difficulty in recovering any additional assets from the at-fault driver. If you are in a serious accident and the at-fault driver only has the minimum coverage, you might receive as little as $15,000, even if your injuries are severe. This is why adequate underinsured motorist coverage is crucial – it protects you in situations where the at-fault driver's insurance falls short.

Of course, if you are hit by an uninsured motorist, you can try to recover damages by finding assets they might own, such as a house. However, it is rare to find significant assets from someone who is uninsured. These individuals often have no job, and typically lack substantial assets. You could also attempt to go after the car owner, but many times, these vehicles have been sold without proper registration, making it difficult to hold the owner accountable.

Here are a couple of typical scenarios that occur when needing to use your UM/UIM insurance.

Scenario 1. Plaintiff if driving and minding his own business when the Defendant does something negligent like run a red light or rear end the Plaintiff. The Defendant has either no insurance or the minimum policy required by law. The Plaintiff has the minimum UM/UIM policy available. The Plaintiff suffers massive injuries including transportation to the hospital, surgery, and post trauma care.

Past medical bills, lost wages, future earnings, future care, and pain and suffering damages easily get into the six figure range. Unfortunately, the Plaintiff will only be able to recover the minimum amount available under his UM or UIM coverage, depending on if the Defendant has insurance. This means that unless we find liability on a third party, such as a government entity, the Plaintiff is left with a fraction of the value of his case.

Scenario 2. Plaintiff is minding his own business, and Defendant does something negligent to injure Plaintiff. The Defendant has a minimum policy. However, in this scenario, the Plaintiff has a higher UM/UIM insurance policy. For the sake of argument, let's say it is twice the minimum. Damages are not too bad, but the case is valued in maybe slightly higher than the Defendant's policy limit.

In addition, to the damages the Defendant caused, the Defendant's insurance company wants to put 50 percent liability on the Plaintiff. So the Defendant's insurance company makes an offer and cuts it in half because of "disputed liability."

The Plaintiff's insurance company comes to the same conclusion my office does and that is that the Defendant is 100 percent liable. Knowing this, we are not going to settle the Defendant's low offer because we have leverage with the Plaintiff's UIM coverage. We know if we can exhaust the Defendant's low coverage, that the Plaintiff's higher coverage will kick in and that Plaintiff's insurance company will not cut the offer in half.

These are two of the most common examples of how UM and UIM insurance affect the recovery of damages for clients. There are many other examples, but the key takeaway is that by insuring you and your family with a higher policy limit, gives us a huge advantage in negotiations and trial preparation.

It is also important to note that your insurance rates typically increase only if you are at fault in an accident, not when you file a claim under your UM or UIM coverage. This coverage is designed to protect you against others and using it should not negatively impact your premiums.

The bottom line is that in today's driving environment, it is vital for you to protect yourself with adequate UM and UIM coverage. With the increasing number of uninsured and underinsured motorists on the road, having this coverage is more important than ever.

CHAPTER 8

WRONGFUL DEATH CLAIMS

The Essence Of A Wrongful Death Claim

A wrongful death claim centers on the death of a person caused by someone else's negligence. These tragic cases often arise in situations like car accidents, where a fatality occurs due to another driver's carelessness or recklessness. No matter how severe the circumstances, what sets a wrongful death claim apart from other legal claims is the unfortunate reality that it must involve the loss of life.

Wrongful Death Claims Vs. "Regular" Personal Injury Claims

The most significant difference between wrongful death claims and regular personal injury claims lies in the value of the claim. A wrongful death claim typically carries a much higher value because it represents the ultimate loss—the loss of life. The compensation sought in these cases reflects the profound and irreversible impact of losing a loved one.

Another key difference is who files the claim. In personal injury cases, the injured person files the claim themselves. However, in wrongful death cases, the claim is filed by the immediate heirs of the deceased—such as a spouse, children, or in some cases, parents or siblings. Depending on the family structure, multiple individuals may be involved in representing the deceased in the claim.

The Value Of A Wrongful Death Case

Maximizing the value in wrongful death cases requires a careful, thorough approach to determine what the case is truly worth. One of the key factors I consider is the future loss of income, especially if the deceased was a spouse. Another crucial aspect is the loss of consortium for married couples—the emotional and relational loss that comes with losing a partner. This process is not easy; it involves analyzing factors like future earnings and inflation. For instance, younger individuals often have more potential earning years ahead, which can increase the claim's value, while older individuals may have fewer future earnings to account for.

Detailed documentation is critical in these cases, just as it is in typical personal injury claims. We meticulously gather comprehensive medical records, employment history, and any other relevant information to substantiate the claim for financial and emotional losses. To navigate these complexities, I also consult with economic experts who can testify about the future value of money, inflation trends, and the broader economic impact. Their insights allow us to make educated estimates about future financial losses.

Ultimately, it is up to a jury to determine the value of a wrongful death case. Our strategy centers on presenting a well-rounded and compelling case that clearly illustrates the profound impact of what has happened. Though while the fundamental approach may be similar to other personal injury cases, the stakes are much higher due to the long-term consequences involved.

Supporting Clients Suffering Through the Loss of a Loved One

Supporting my clients through the loss of a loved one is, without a doubt, one of the most challenging parts of handling wrongful death claims – it is also one of the most important. Grief manifests in many forms, whether the loss is of a spouse, a parent mourning a child, or a child left without a parent. Understanding this is one thing, but being there for my clients as they navigate these emotions is another. That is why I always make it a priority to offer resources on grief and, more importantly, to be there for them in whatever way they need and let them know they are not alone.

I remember a case where a child's death was due to a school's negligence—a tragedy that left an indelible mark on the family. The emotional toll on the family was staggering, and it was heartbreaking to witness their intense sorrow and anger. In situations like these, my role extends far beyond that of a lawyer—I strive to provide a steadying force, helping my clients manage their emotions while guiding them through the legal process. In these cases, my role is not just about offering legal counsel; it is about being an anchor for people in their darkest hours.

Putting a value on a lost loved one is a nearly impossible task. How can one quantify the life of a child or a spouse of 30 years? The truth is, you cannot. Yet, the legal system demands a number - a cold, calculated figure that somehow encapsulates a life that was once priceless.

This is where my role becomes even more crucial, talking through the difficult conversations that my clients might not be ready to face. For instance, many people feel like the lawsuit is a way to keep their loved one's memory alive. The case often becomes a major part of their life, and when it ends, it marks a time where someone is faced with finding a new way to move forward.

Understanding this, I make it my mission to ensure that the emotional weight of their loss isn't overshadowed by the legal process. My goal is to guide the people I work with through the legal maze while respecting the profound personal impact it has on their lives. I take this responsibility very seriously; it is not something I handle lightly.

Carrying the emotional burden of your clients is something you learn to handle day by day. Grief is unpredictable—one day, a client might seem okay, and the next, they might feel like they overcome with grief. The best approach is patience. I do everything in my power to show up for my clients to the best of my ability and adapt to whatever emotions they are experiencing on any given day.

As the case concludes, people respond in different ways. Some are ready for closure and eager to move on, while others might hesitate, fearing that the end of the lawsuit means they must truly say goodbye.

It is a significant transition—almost like a rite of passage toward the next chapter of their lives.

Some clients are very emotional, seeking comfort through tears and a hug, while others are more reserved, ready to move on quietly. There is no one right way to react. It is important to remember that each person's response is unique. For me, the key to handling this burden is recognizing that there is no single approach to supporting clients through their grief. Like each person I work with, every case is different, and so is every emotional journey. The best you can do is to perform for people to the best of your ability and take things one day at a time.

CHAPTER 9

PRACTICAL TIPS & CLOSING REMARKS

How To Find The Right Attorney

As I have emphasized throughout this book, when it comes to personal injury claims, contacting an experienced attorney as soon as possible is crucial. The sooner you have professional guidance, the better your chances of successfully navigating the complexities of your case. But how do you find the right attorney? It is not just about finding someone with a law degree—it is about finding someone who aligns with your needs and is equipped to handle your case.

The most important factor to consider when choosing a personal injury attorney is finding someone you can connect with and communicate with easily. If you do not feel comfortable with an attorney for any reason, it is okay to keep looking. You need someone with whom you can have open, honest conversations. Clear communication is the foundation of a strong client-attorney relationship, and it is essential that you understand why certain steps are being taken and the reasoning behind them.

Trust is key. You need to feel confident that your attorney is looking out for your best interests in everything that is done. This is especially important because you might only hire an attorney once or twice in your life, and when you do, you are entrusting them with something incredibly significant—not just a case, but a part of your life. That is why reputation matters. Choose someone with a solid track record, someone who has proven they can deliver results.

When you find an attorney you trust and can communicate with effectively, you have taken a big step toward ensuring a successful partnership. From my perspective, these qualities—trust and communication—are more important than any other factor in achieving a positive outcome for your case.

Look For Someone With Unique Qualifications

My experience as a traffic investigator offers a unique advantage when representing clients in personal injury cases. Investigating traffic incidents requires a deep understanding of the vehicle code, fault determination, and the nuances of negligence. This background allows me to identify comparative negligence, where both parties may share some degree of fault, which can be critical in negotiating and arguing for a favorable outcome.

Many attorneys, despite years of experience, often miss fundamental aspects of the vehicle code and liability issues. They might handle cases in a routine manner, overlooking important details that are crucial to your case. My experience provides a different perspective, empowering me to dissect accident reports with an understanding of the investigator's thought process. This allows for a more thorough analysis and a stronger representation of your interests.

Delivering Results

To me, nothing is impossible. Challenging? Absolutely. But impossible? That is a whole different story. I remember a case where the insurance company flat-out refused to engage with us, saying, "We're not going to talk to you until you file a lawsuit." My immediate thought was, "*Oh yeah?* I'll take care of that." So, we filed the lawsuit. Although it took several years, we eventually reached mediation. Even then, their initial offer to our client was a pittance.

But we did not back down. We kept pushing forward, and just a month or two before the trial, they came back with a multiple seven-figure offer, which our client ultimately accepted. We went from a zero offer to a high seven-figure settlement. If the injured party did not have an attorney, who knows how things might have played out? To me, it was a clear-cut case of liability, but the insurance company did not see it that way.

The key issue was that they tried to pin the blame on someone else entirely, claiming it wasn't their fault. This is a classic case of comparative negligence. Even if someone else shares some of the blame, that does not erase your own liability. In this case, the insurance company wouldn't even begin discussions until we filed a lawsuit. Once we did, we could start taking depositions and gathering records—steps that ultimately turned the case around.

In another instance, I represented a client who was driving a classic car that did not require seat belts. The insurance company argued that he was responsible for his injuries because he was not wearing a seat belt. Not surprisingly, they offered us nothing, insisting the client was responsible for his own injuries. However, I knew that a specific vehicle code exempts classic cars from the seat belt requirement. Despite their zero-dollar offer, we went to arbitration and won a six-figure settlement.

These cases illustrate that sometimes, the only way to secure a fair settlement is to fight back with deep knowledge of the law and the specifics of your case. While these are not things clients can usually handle on their own, I am proud to assist as a lawyer who can navigate these complex situations and ensure that my clients get the full amount of compensation that they truly deserve.

Concluding Thoughts

If there is one thing I hope you take away from this book, it is a deeper understanding of what we do as personal injury attorneys and why we do it. We work in a niche area of the law that most people never have to navigate—and, hopefully, never will. The reality is that in the vast majority of cases, you are far better off with professional representation than trying to manage things on your own. There are countless details that can make or break a case, and these are the things an attorney handles every day.

The main message I want to convey is this: My goal is always to put you in a better position than you would be if you hired someone else or tried to handle your case alone. By choosing my firm and placing your trust in us, my aim is to ensure you come out ahead—not just in terms of your settlement but in your overall experience.

Your success is our success. Your best interests will *always* be our top priority.

INDEX

A

accident reconstructionist · 48
at-fault driver · 53
attorney-client privilege · 20

C

claim · 32
claims adjuster · 30
comparative negligence · 67
comprehensive medical records · 60
concussions · 39

D

damage · 17
demand package · 35
discovery · 47

E

evidence · 16
Evidence Eradication Team · 16

F

fault · 18

H

health insurance company · 23

I

insurance company · 24

J

jurors · 36

L

liability · 18

M

mediation · 47
medical attention · 17
medical records · 34
medical treatment · 22
Medicare · 42

N

noneconomic damages · 40

P

pain and suffering · 40
personal injury attorney · 27
personal injury claim · 38
personal injury law · 23
plaintiff · 33
police report · 28

S

settlement conference · 47
subrogation claims · 23

T

traumatic brain injuries · 39
trial · 46
two-year statute of limitations · 33

U

UIM coverage · 54

Underinsured Motorist · 53
Uninsured Motorist · 53

W

wrongful death claim · 58

NOTES

Made in the USA
Monee, IL
05 November 2026

67387963R00048